The Second Battle of Fallujah: The History of the Biggest Battle of the Iraq War

By Charles River Editors

A picture of U.S. Marines during the battle in November 2004

About Charles River Editors

Charles River Editors is a boutique digital publishing company, specializing in bringing history back to life with educational and engaging books on a wide range of topics. Keep up to date with our new and free offerings with this 5 second sign up on our weekly mailing list, and visit Our Kindle Author Page to see other recently published Kindle titles.

We make these books for you and always want to know our readers' opinions, so we encourage you to leave reviews and look forward to publishing new and exciting titles each week.

Introduction

A picture of Marines planning to enter a building during the battle

The Second Battle of Fallujah

"I am scared to death that they [the war hawks in Washington] are going to convince the president that they can do this overthrow of Saddam on the cheap, and we'll find ourselves in the middle of a swamp because we didn't plan to do it the right way." - Lawrence Eagleburger, former Secretary of State

"Some of the heaviest urban combat U.S. Marines have been involved in since the Battle of Hué City in Vietnam in 1968." – The U.S. military's description of the battle

The city of Fallujah is located in Iraq's western Anbar Province, approximately 65 kilometers west of Baghdad, the country's capital. Its history, along with the history of Iraq (whose modern borders are part of what was once known as Mesopotamia), goes back thousands of years, and the country's modern history played a strong role in shaping the fighting in and around Fallujah in 2004.

Moreover, as the name of the battle implies, no description of the fighting for Fallujah is as straightforward as it may sound. In fact, there have been multiple battles for Fallujah over a span of many years, including Operation Vigilant Resolve in April 2004 (also referred to as the "First Battle of Fallujah"), Operation Al Fajr and Operation Phantom Fury (the Second Battle of Fallujah, which commenced in November of the same year), the February 2014 capture of the city by the then-Islamic State of Iraq and al-Sham (ISIS, which later changed its name to Islamic State), and the 2016 Iraqi-led offensive to clear ISIS from the city.

The most famous of these was certainly the Second Battle, but no history about the fighting can focus solely on the events from November to December 2004, which covered the beginning and conclusion of the operations. In order to understand the offensive, it is important to understand the conditions that soldiers in combat faced, as well as the events and perceptions that helped create these conditions, including the attitudes of local residents in Fallujah, the events that contributed to the First Battle of Fallujah, the lead-up to the second battle, the ramifications for the rest of the country, and the creation of al-Qaeda in Iraq. Given the fact that fighting across Iraq is still ongoing over a decade later, it's safe to characterize the Second Battle of Fallujah had and continues to have a major influence over the evolution of the Iraq War.

The Second Battle of Fallujah: The History of the Biggest Battle of the Iraq War looks at the battle widely considered to be the heaviest fighting of the conflict. Along with pictures of important people, places, and events, you will learn about the battle like never before.

The Second Battle of Fallujah: The History of the Biggest Battle of the Iraq War

About Charles River Editors

Introduction

Chapter 1: The Start of the Iraq War

Chapter 2: The City of Fallujah

Chapter 3: The First Battle of Fallujah

Chapter 4: Al-Qaeda in Iraq

Chapter 5: The Second Battle of Fallujah

Chapter 6: The Impact and Aftermath of the Battle

Online Resources

Bibliography

Free Books by Charles River Editors

Discounted Books by Charles River Editors

Chapter 1: The Start of the Iraq War

Just hours after the terrorist attacks on 9/11, President George W. Bush stood before a shocked and devastated nation and vowed that the U.S. would respond to the terrorist attacks that occurred that day, and that Washington would make "no distinction between those who planned these acts and those who harbor them." His intention was clear – the American government will not only punish those who perpetrated the attacks, but also anyone and everyone who harbored, aided, or abetted the terrorists.[1]

On the morning of September 17, 2001, President Bush agreed with his core advisors that Afghanistan would be the singular focus of the initial U.S. response to the 9/11 attacks. Bush had been intent on attacking Iraq at first, but the lack of evidence of Saddam Hussein's involvement led many of his advisors to push for an invasion of Afghanistan instead of Iraq. However, less than two months later, Bush again shifted his focus back to Hussein and secretly ordered the Joint Chiefs of Staff to initiate plans to depose him.[2] In his State of the Union address on January 29, 2002, Bush began to publicly push for the nation's attention to shift to Iraq, which he famously labeled as one of the countries making up the "axis of evil" that was allegedly supporting terrorism and posing a grave danger to U.S. national security. He followed this with what is now notoriously known as an utterly unsubstantiated claim and one of the Bush administration's biggest blunders: that Iraq was in possession of weapons of mass destruction (WMDs).[3] Thus emerged what has popularly become known as the Bush Doctrine, a term first coined by Charles Krauthammer to describe the Bush administration's unilateral foreign policy, centered on the idea that "either you are with us or you are with the terrorists."[4]

Though Bush is understandably blamed for what has taken place in Iraq in the 21st century, an interest in regime change in Iraq can be traced long before the 2003 invasion. Under the administration of former President Bill Clinton, the Iraq Liberation Act of 1998 was passed. "It should be the policy of the United States", states the legislation, "to support efforts to remove the regime headed by Saddam Hussein from power in Iraq and to promote the emergence of a democratic government to replace that regime".[5] The Republican Party's 2000 platform, moreover, specifically mentioned Iraq and the removal of Hussein from power. "A new administration", "it states, will react forcefully and unequivocally to any evidence of reconstituted Iraqi capabilities for producing weapons of mass destruction". The platform further explains that the Iraq Liberation Act "should be regarded as a starting point in a comprehensive plan for the removal of Saddam Hussein".[6]

---

[1] Jon Western, *Selling Intervention and War: The Presidency, the Media, and the American Public* (Baltimore: The John Hopkins University Press, 2005), 175.

[2] Tommy Franks, *American Soldier General Tommy Franks* (New York: Regan Books, 2004), 315.

[3] George W. Bush, "The President's State of the Union Address" (speech, Washington DC, January 29, 2002), The White House Archives, http://georgewbush-whitehouse.archives.gov/news/releases/2002/01/20020129-11.html.

[4] Charles Krauthammer, "Charlie Gibson's Gaffe," *The Washington Post,* September 13, 2008, http://www.washingtonpost.com/wp-dyn/content/article/2008/09/12/AR2008091202457.html.

[5] "Iraq Liberation Act of 1998", H.R. 4655, 105th Congress, 2nd session.

In October of 2002, just over a year after 9/11, Bush received the support of nearly three-fourths of the Congress for a resolution authorizing him to use any means necessary against Iraq – an amendment called the Join Resolution to Authorize the Use of United States Armed Forces against Iraq. Six months after that, in March 2003, Bush ordered the launch of what was being called a preventive war to unseat Hussein. Polls taken during this time show that Bush enjoyed widespread public support, partly due to the administration's elaborate domestic public relations campaign to market the war to its people. It was shown that in February 2003, a staggering 64% of Americans supported military action to remove Saddam Hussein from power.[7]

There was still no evidence of Saddam Hussein's complicity in the events of September 11, but the Bush administration led a coalition of forces that invaded Iraq in March 2003 and deposed Saddam Hussein at lightning speed. On March 18 2003, shrugging off fierce condemnation by the United Nations (UN), the U.S. began its bombing campaign in Iraq, joined by forces from the U.K., Spain, Italy, Poland, Australia, and Denmark. On March 19 of that year, Bush announced that, "on [his] orders, coalition forces have begun striking selected targets of military importance to undermine Saddam Hussein's ability to wage war". He continued on to explain that these actions were the "opening stages of what will be a broad and concerted campaign". The aim was to remove Saddam Hussein, described by Bush as "an outlaw regime that threatens the peace with weapons of mass murder".[8]

The weapons referenced were weapons of mass destruction (WMDs). In United Nations Security Council (UNSC) Resolution 1441 of November 2002, it was determined that the country "ha[d] been and remain[ed] in material breach of its obligations [...], in particular through Iraq's failure to cooperate with United Nations inspectors and the IAEA [International Atomic Energy Agency]".[9] This referred primarily to UNSC Resolution 687, which was passed in April 1991 and set the terms with which Iraq must comply following its loss in Operation Desert Storm after it invaded Kuwait, often referred to as the first Gulf War. As part of these terms, Saddam Hussein was to remove and destroy all chemical and biological weapons, as well as ballistic missiles with ranges of over 150 km (approximately 93 miles), and allow for on-site inspections of these capabilities. It further stipulated that Iraq reaffirm its commitment to the Nuclear Non-Proliferation Treaty (NPT) and "unconditionally agree not to acquire or develop nuclear weapons or nuclear-weapons-usable material or any subsystems or components or any research, development, support or manufacturing facilities related to the above".[10]

In February 2003, in a speech to the UNSC, then Secretary of State Colin Powell referenced Resolution 1441 and stated that Saddam Hussein "made no effort [...] to disarm as required by

[6] "Republican Platform 2000", CNN.
[7] Bootie Cosgrove-Mather, "Poll: Talk First, Fight Later," CBS News, January 23, 2003,
    http://www.cbsnews.com/news/poll-talk-first-fight-later/.
[8] "President Bush Addresses the Nation", The White House President George W. Bush, 19 March 2003.
[9] United Nations Security Council, "Resolution 1441 (2002)", 8 November 2002.
[10] United Nations Security Council, "Resolution 687 (1991), 8 April 1991.

the international community". Rather, Powell explained, "the facts and Iraq's behavior show that Saddam Hussein and his regime are concealing their efforts to produce more weapons of mass destruction". He then provided evidence to this effect, regarding both chemical and nuclear weapons.[11] Moreover, the ability to use force was included under the auspices of Resolution 1441, which declared that it was "acting under Chapter VII of the Charter of the United Nations". Chapter VII allows for the use of force (Article 42) if non-military actions (Article 41) "have proved to be inadequate".[12]

---

[11] "Full text of Colin Powell's speech", *The Guardian*, 5 February 2003.
[12] "Charter of the United Nations: Chapter VII: Actions with respect to threats to the peace, breaches of the peace, and acts of aggression", *United Nations*.

Powell

This was the rationale for the use of force in Iraq, alongside the ties Powell made between Hussein and al-Qaeda, the Sunni militant jihadist group responsible for the September 11, 2001 attacks against the World Trade Center in New York and Pentagon in Washington, D.C. The link between the two was a man named Abu Musab al-Zarqawi (who will be discussed in more detail further below). Powell stated to the UN Security Council: "Iraq today harbors a deadly terrorist network headed by Abu Musab Al-Zarqawi, an associate and collaborator of Osama bin Laden and his Al Qaeda lieutenants. When our coalition ousted the Taliban, the Zarqawi network helped establish another poison and explosive training center camp. And this camp is located in northeastern Iraq. He traveled to Baghdad in May 2002 for medical treatment, staying in the capital of Iraq for two months while he recuperated to fight another day. During this stay, nearly two dozen extremists converged on Baghdad and established a base of operations there. These Al Qaeda affiliates, based in Baghdad, now coordinate the movement of people, money and supplies into and throughout Iraq for his network, and they've now been operating freely in the capital for more than eight months. We asked a friendly security service to approach Baghdad about extraditing Zarqawi and providing information about him and his close associates. This service contacted Iraqi officials twice, and we passed details that should have made it easy to find Zarqawi. The network remains in Baghdad."[13]

Analysts have since concluded that the statement made by Powell was false, because at the time of his statement in February of 2003, there were no significant ties between bin Laden and al-Zarqawi that indicated an extensive relationship, nor was there any evidence that Powell presented that proved al-Zarqawi to be one of bin Laden's top commanders. It was only over a year and a half later, in December 2004, that bin Laden named al-Zarqawi the *emir* (commander or leader) of an al-Qaeda branch in Iraq. A 2006 Senate Report on the intelligence gathered about Iraq before the war also concluded, "Postwar information indicates that Saddam Hussein attempted, unsuccessfully, to locate and capture al-Zarqawi and that the regime did not have a relationship with, harbor, or turn a blind eye toward Zarqawi."

---

[13] Loretta Napoleoni, "Profile of a Killer," *Foreign Policy,* November 9, 2005,
http://www.foreignpolicy.com/articles/2005/11/09/profile_of_a_killer?page=0,2&hidecomments=yes.

Abu Musab al-Zarqawi

The 2003 Iraq war is much criticized. One of the main critiques regards the reliability of the intelligence used as rationale for the invasion, as well as the extent of knowledge of those, like Powell, who repeated this intelligence. While it is now well-known that Iraq didn't have any weapons of mass destruction ready for use, an October 2014 article in *The New York Times* revealed the presence of chemical weapons in Iraq. These were, according to the piece, "remnants of an arms program Iraq had rushed into production in the 1980s during the Iran-Iraq war" and not a program that had been recently in progress.[14]

Perhaps one of the most frequently repeated pieces of criticism, however, relates to the premature May 1, 2003 speech by Bush that has been dubbed the "mission accomplished" speech due to the banner behind the former president that displayed these words. In the speech, he declared that "major combat operations in Iraq [had] ended" and that "Iraq is free". Although he would also state that there was still "difficult work to do in Iraq", the subsequent phase was described as involving reconstruction and a transition to democracy.[15] As it turned out, "major combat operations" were not over and, in fact, the fighting for Fallujah occurred six months after Bush declared that the U.S. mission in Iraq had been accomplished.

---

[14] C.J. Chivers, "The Secret Casualties of Iraq's Abandoned Chemical Weapons", *The New York Times*, 14 October 2014. The Iran-Iraq war refers to an eight-year conflict between the two countries that began in September 1980 with Iraq's invasion of Iran.

[15] For the full text of the speech, see "Bush makes historic speech aboard warship", *CNN*, 2 May 2003.

A picture of the U.S.S *Abraham Lincoln* **with the famous banner**

A picture of President Bush on the ship before the Mission Accomplished speech

If anything, the fall of Baghdad also triggered the outbreak of regional and sectarian violence throughout the country. It was the single biggest indication that Saddam's reign was over, a signal to the dozens of various independent militant groups across the country that now that Saddam was in hiding, they were now free to carve out their own territories and amass power. Old grudges and new ambitions made way for fresh fighting, and the U.S. and Coalition forces quickly found themselves in the midst of a potential civil war. U.S. forces swiftly ordered the immediate cessation of hostilities and announced that Baghdad was to remain the capital, but while militant groups temporarily halted their fighting, tensions had already risen to the point of no return.

Chapter 2: The City of Fallujah

A map of Iraq

A picture of Fallujah taken during the fighting in November 2004

Fallujah is Anbar Province's largest city; prior to the 2003 invasion its population was estimated at between 250,000 and 400,000 people.[16] Notably and importantly, the city is majority Sunni and was a main area of support for Saddam Hussein. In fact, it is part of what is known as the "Sunni Triangle", which refers to an area housing a majority Sunni population. The "triangle" can more or less be drawn with Ramadi (located west of Fallujah), Baghdad, and Tikrit at its three corners.[17]

There are three key characteristics that helped mold the response of Fallujah's inhabitants to foreign intervention. This includes Saddam Hussein's patronage system among its Sunni majority population, a strong tribal identity, and the city's religious conservatism. Firstly, its population extensively benefited from the country's Sunni leadership and often filled the ranks of the military, police, and intelligence. This also meant that, after the 2003 invasion when the security forces were disbanded, a large portion of the population found themselves unemployed and without income. The disbanding, wrote Mark Thompson in *TIME Magazine*, "drove many of the suddenly out-of-work Sunni warriors into alliances with a Sunni insurgency that would eventually mutate into ISIS".[18]

---

[16] The current population is unclear, particularly given the 2016 Iraqi-led offensive to recapture the city from ISIS. There are large numbers of displaced persons and return to ISIS-held cities can take a significant amount of time, due to the destruction, as well as the number of IEDs and booby-traps left behind by the militant group.

[17] Ahmed S. Hashim, *Insurgency and Counter-insurgency in Iraq* (New York: Cornell University Press, 2006), p. 129.

[18] Mark Thompson, "How Disbanding the Iraqi Army Fueled ISIS", *TIME Magazine*, 28 May 2015.

Moreover, de-Ba'athification, which refers to the policy that aimed to remove the influence of Saddam Hussein's Ba'ath Party in Iraq's post-Saddam political system, also impacted employment prospects for his Sunni supporters in Fallujah. Although rescinded in June 2004 upon transfer of authority to Iraqi Interim Government,[19] this policy implemented an investigation, identification, and appeal process that identified and barred "Ba'ath Party affiliations of employees at all ministries".[20] In other words, the invasion of Iraq and subsequent policies pursued as a result of the invasion caused the population of Fallujah to see their existing wages, employment, and political power, as well as their potential job and income opportunities, sharply decline.

---

[19] L. Paul Bremer, "Coalition Provisional Authority Order Number 100: Transition of Laws, Regulations, Orders, and Directives Issued by the Coalition Provisional Authority", 28 June 2004, p. 4.

[20] L. Paul Bremer, "Iraq Coalition Provincial Authority Order Number One, De-Ba'athification of Iraqi Society", 16 May 2003.

Hussein

In addition to the patronage system, Fallujah's population is considered to be religiously conservative, with clerics playing an important role in local affairs and the city containing a large number of religious schools and colleges. The city also boasted such a large number of mosques that it was given the moniker "city of mosques".

In fact, the city's religious climate at times served as a point of contention with the Saddam Hussein regime. Roel Meijer, an expert in Islamist and Salafi movements at the Netherlands Institute of International Relations, argues that there was an absence of Fallujah residents from the highest positions in the Ba'ath Party and Republican Guards, the elite troops from the Iraqi Army that reported directly to Saddam Hussein, due in part to the city's religious conservatism.

Many of Fallujah's religious leaders, Meijer explains, "sympathized with the banned Muslim Brotherhood and especially some of the youthful members of the tribes had Salafi ties". [21] Salafism refers to a conservative movement, which argues that authentic Islam can only be found in the "lived example of the early, righteous generations of the *Salaf*, who were closest in both time and proximity to the Prophet Muhammad".[22] Ahmed Hashim, the author of *Insurgency and Counter-insurgency in Iraq*, argues that its popularity in Fallujah rose in the 1990s. Meijer, meanwhile, notes that Saddam Hussein even had some male children of tribal leaders "executed to demonstrate his intolerance for dissent".[23]

As a result, there were a number of religious figures in Fallujah who supported and extolled resistance to the invasion from almost the very beginning, including in their sermons. The imam of Fallujah's Khaleed ibn Walid Mosque, for example, reportedly praised a May 2003 attack in the city.[24] In June, another stated that if the foreign troops[25] "try to change our ways, we will wage *jihad* against them and die holy deaths for our people".[26]

The third and final characteristic is the strong tribal identity and related values prevalent among the population. According to Meijer, the majority of Fallujah residents "belong to six tribal clans who have kept alive typical tribal traditions". This includes "mutual support and solidarity, a certain lifestyle, certain values such as a strong sense of honour, blood revenge and the concept of women as the embodiment of family and clan honour".[27]

Chapter 3: The First Battle of Fallujah

The story of Fallujah during the Iraq War truly begins approximately one year prior to the first battle of Fallujah. Initially, there was no foreign presence in Fallujah, but this changed at the end of April 2003, about one month after Iraq was invaded, when American troops finally entered the city. At this point, apprehension was already high; some Sunni clerics reportedly "warned that the Americans would turn the city over to the Shi'a, and Iraq over to Israel".[28]

Not long after, on April 28, a protest was held outside the al-Qa'id primary school, which had

---

[21] Roel Meijer, "'Defending our Honor': Authenticity and the Faming of Resistance in the Iraqi Sunni Town of Falluja", *Etnofoon*, Vol. 17 (2004): pp. 26-7.

[22] Shadi Hamid and Rashid Dar, "Islamism, Salafism, and jihadism: A primer", *The Brookings Institute*, 15 July 2016. Salafists (or Islamists) cannot be confused with militant Sunni Islamist/jihadist groups like al-Qaeda and the so-called Islamic State. While the latter can and often are both Islamists and Salafists, these elements should be distinguished by their calls for violence to be used against their enemy.

[23] Meijer, "'Defending our Honor'", p. 27.

[24] Hashim, *Insurgency and Counter-insurgency in Iraq*, p. 28.

[25] For the purposes of this paper, troops that were part of the U.S.-led invasion of Iraq in 2003 will be referred to as U.S. or coalition troops. In terms of those opposing their invasion, these groups will be referred to as insurgents, anti-U.S. fighters, or by their name or ideological affiliation.

[26] Meijer, "'Defending our Honor'", p. 29.

[27] Ibid, p. 26.

[28] Martha L. Cottam and Joe W. Huseby, *Confronting Al Qaeda: The Sunni Awakening and American Strategy in Al Anbar* (Maryland, Rowman & Littlefield: 2016), p. 42.

been converted to a U.S. base, demanding that U.S. forces leave. In what would ultimately become a disputed event, soldiers opened fire on protesters, claiming that they were returning gunfire from the crowd. Others accounts asserted that the soldiers fired without provocation, disputing the claim that the initial gunfire came from the crowd.[29] One report even alleged that the vast majority of participants were teachers and relatives of the school's students, who were also demonstrating against its takeover as a military base.[30] According to a report from Human Rights Watch (HRW) released the following June, which includes interviews with residents, local officials, and members of the U.S. military, 17 people were killed and over 70 injured in the dispersal. Other sources, including from *The New York Times*, puts the number of dead at 15.[31] The HRW report states that "the physical evidence at the school does not support claims of an effective attack on the building as described by U.S. troops". This finding was based upon the lack of bullet damage to the structure from where soldiers opened fire.[32]

Two days later, on April 30, protesters were again fired upon. According to reports, hundreds of people marched down the city's main street to a compound housing the battalion headquarters for the 82nd Airborne Division of the U.S. Army. Accounts then describe soldiers opening fire after protesters began throwing rocks and shoes at the compound. The U.S. denied opening fire without provocation, stating that a six-vehicle convoy came under gunfire, which was then returned.[33] According to HRW's report, three people were killed and at least 16 injured in the incident.[34]

In addition to the response against protesters, U.S. soldiers were perceived by residents as disrespectful to their religion, culture and values. HRW's report cited various allegations, received via interviews with local residents and officials, such as claims that soldiers were conducting "aggressive street patrols" and, more offensively, "inappropriately eyeing Iraqi women". One of the issues was the use of binoculars and night-vision: Soldiers surveying the inhabitants from rooftops was seen as an invasion of privacy.[35] Meijer further noted that one action that was regarded as especially offensive and contrary to local values occurred during house-to-house searches. "If the man they were looking for had escaped", he explains, "They would take a female member of the family as hostage".[36] Recalling the importance of women to

---

[29] "Violent Response: The U.S. Army in al-Falluja", *Human Rights Watch*, 16 June 2003 and Ian Fisher, "U.S. Troops Fire on Iraqi Protesters, leaving 15 dead", *The New York Times*, 29 April 2003.
[30] Peace Direct and Oxford Research Group, "Learning from Fallujah: Lessons identified 2003-2005", *Peace Direct* (2005): pp. 4-5.
[31] "Violent Response", *Human Rights Watch*.
[32] Ibid. This report presents both sides and it is recommended to read this report in full for a more detailed presentation of the incidents. It does, for example, note that the city's mayor "collected information in the town that supporters of Saddam Hussein provoked a conflict by shooting at the U.S. troops based at the school". This paper does not intend to argue either side but, rather, demonstrate that, regardless of who was responsible, this incident helped stoke further anger toward the U.S. presence in Fallujah.
[33] George Wright and agencies, "U.S. troops 'shoot dead two more Iraqis'", *The Guardian*, 30 April 2003.
[34] "Violent Response", *Human Rights Watch*.
[35] Ibid and Meijer, "'Defending our Honor'", p. 28.
[36] Meijer, "'Defending our Honor'", p. 28.

family and clan honor, these actions help fuel resentment among the local population toward the invading forces. This was on top of anger toward arrests in general.

Although not specifically referring to Fallujah but, rather, Iraq as a whole, the International Committee of the Red Cross (ICRC) released a report in 2004 on the treatment of detainees by coalition forces. The following is an excerpt of this report: "Arrests as described in these allegations tended to follow a pattern. Arresting authorities entered houses usually after dark, breaking down doors, waking up residents roughly, yelling orders, forcing family members into one room under military guard while searching the rest of the house and further breaking doors, cabinets and other property. They arrested suspects, tying their hands in the back with flexi-cuffs, hooding them, and taking them away. Sometimes they arrested all adult males present in a house, including elderly, handicapped or sick people. Treatment often included pushing people around, insulting them, taking aim with rifles, punching and kicking and striking with rifles. Individuals were often led away in whatever they happened to be wearing at the time of the arrest—sometimes in pyjamas [sic] or underwear—and were denied the opportunity to gather a few essential belongings, such as clothing, hygiene items, medicine or eyeglasses."[37]

For a culture that particularly emphasized honor, this was surely deemed as a humiliation, which was a common perception among Iraqis. In fact, in a March 2004 *ABC News* poll cited by a Peace Direct and Oxford Research Group report, "42 percent of Iraqis thought the war had liberated Iraq, while 41 percent that it had humiliated Iraq".[38] Made worse were figures cited by the ICRC on the accurate identification of individuals deemed to be threats: In their report, the humanitarian group cited military intelligence officers who estimated that between 70 and 90 percent of those detained in Iraq "had been arrested by mistake". [39] For locals, it was one thing to be humiliated during an arrest, and it was quite another to be humiliated because of a mistake. Moreover, there were serious delays in the notifications of detentions to family members, with some reports stating that the notifications never came at all. The ICRC also detailed multiple accusations regarding the "ill-treatment" of detainees during interrogation and holding.[40] Residents could not see these actions as those of a "liberator".

It must also be noted here that the accuracy of any of these allegations and the rationale behind such policies, such as the use of binoculars and the detention of women, are in some ways irrelevant to the situation. After all, even if none of that had actually taken place, it is the perception of the local residents that is the pertinent factor since it was the driver for opposition and dissatisfaction. The fact is that the response to demonstrators, along with the impressions of

[37] "Report of the International Committee of the Red Cross (ICRC) on the Treatment by the Coalition Forces of Prisoners of War and Other Protected Persons by the Geneva Conventions in Iraq During Arrest, Internment and Interrogation", *ICRC*, February 2004, p. 7.
[38] Peace Direct and Oxford Research Group, "Learning from Fallujah", p. 7.
[39] "On the Treatment by the Coalition Forces of Prisoners of War", *ICRC*, pp. 8-9.
[40] "On the Treatment by the Coalition Forces of Prisoners of War", *ICRC*, p. 9. For more information on the treatment of detainees, see pp. 9-22.

the foreign troops and their actions, contributed to the rise of opposition to their presence within Fallujah and the multiple attacks witnessed in the following months against U.S. forces stationed in and around the city.

On the night of the April 30 demonstration mentioned above, for example, seven soldiers were injured when a grenade was thrown into a U.S. base. A U.S. military spokesman, Captain Alan Vaught, even described this incident specifically as revenge.[41] On May 27, U.S. soldiers in armored vehicles that were manning a checkpoint in Fallujah came under attack by fighters with rocket-propelled grenades (RPGs).[42] A month later, on June 30, an explosion occurred at a mosque in Fallujah, with locals placing blame on the U.S. for what they described as a missile or airstrike. The U.S. rejected these accusations: Sergeant Thomas McMurty, a member of the 346th tactical psychological operations company, told the Associated Press (AP) that "there is no evidence that it was anything else but a ground-based explosive".[43] However, as previously noted, it is the perception among locals, even if factually incorrect, that influenced the situation on the ground.

Meanwhile, in October, an ambush on U.S. troops in central Fallujah near the mayor's office triggered a firefight that saw one person killed and four others wounded, two of whom were civilians and one of whom was a local police officer.[44] Toward the end of that month, a car bomb also detonated on a main street approximately 100 feet from a school and 330 feet from a police station, killing at least four.[45] And at the beginning of November, a U.S. Army Chinook helicopter that was transporting troops out of the country for leave was shot down near Fallujah.[46]

All the while, U.S. forces attempted to improve relations with the local population during this period, even if they failed to notably alter how they were viewed. Soldiers may have provided food, books, medicine, and toys to local residents, but there were side-by-side policies that failed to inspire confidence, including one that saw the confiscation of privately owned motorcycles and other vehicles.[47] Efforts to provide explanations for certain actions also failed to change perceptions. For example, following a June 15 raid which saw 1,300 U.S. soldiers supported by helicopters conduct arrest raids, including in farmhouses in the northwestern outskirts, members of the psychological operations team drove through the city explaining via loudspeaker the rationale for the raid.[48] However, there were also large numbers of arrests across the city, with

---

[41] Staff and agencies, "Falluja grenade attack injures U.S. soldiers", *The Guardian*, 1 May 2003.
[42] Rory McCarthy, "Two U.S. soldiers killed", *The Guardian*, 28 May 2003.
[43] Agencies, "U.S. soldiers injured in series of attacks", *The Guardian*, 1 July 2003.
[44] Alex Berenson, "The Struggle for Iraq: Combat; U.S. Soldiers Are Ambushed By Guerrillas in Iraqi Town", *The New York Times*, 3 October 2003.
[45] Joel Roberts, "U.S. Tank Hit, 2 GIs dead in Iraq", *CBS News*, 29 October 2003.
[46] Steven Komarow, "Chopper shot down in Iraq, killing 16 GIs", *U.S.A Today*, 2 November 2003.
[47] William Head, "The Battles of Al-Fallujah: Urban Warfare and the Growing Roles of Airpower", *Virginia Review of Asian Studies*, Vol. 18 (2016): p. 117 (originally published in *Air Power History*, Vol. 60, No. 4 (Winter 2013): pp. 32-51) and Rory McCarthy, "Policing Iraqis tests U.S. troops", *The Guardian*, 16 June 2003.
[48] Rory McCarthy, "Policing Iraqis tests U.S. troops", *The Guardian*, 16 June 2003.

many of the detainees released without charge. In the minds of those who were held and then released, along with their family and friends, explanations that only "wanted men" were the target of arrest operations could not change any hearts or minds. In other words, actions spoke louder than words.

Meijer describes the discourse among those opposing the U.S. presence as a combination of tribal, nationalist, and religious rhetoric. He further notes the evolution from unorganized operations focused primarily on "fulfilling their duty for blood revenge" to a much more organized resistance with broader support among the population and religious leaders by the end of 2003. This included some of the more moderate clerics who had initially called for restraint.[49] Meijer's description would sharply contrast to the manner in which those resisting the U.S. presence were described: as former members of the Ba'ath Party and Saddam Hussein loyalists, criminals that had been purposely released by Iraq's former leader prior to the invasion, and foreign fighters.[50] Although the U.S. government, as well as the interim Iraqi government, would attempt to distinguish between the insurgents and the population, the fact remained that there was real support on the ground for those resisting U.S. troops. According to a local doctor quoted by *The Guardian*, few people were interested in criticizing the fighters, emphasizing the relatively extensive opposition to the U.S. presence in the city.[51] Officials from both the local and federal government would also publicly criticize actions taken in Fallujah.

Toward the end of 2003 and beginning of 2004, as the opposition became more organized, the situation in Fallujah deteriorated and the violence escalated. Fighters opposed to the U.S. intervention were increasingly able to improve their ability to respond and target coalition operations, making their attacks deadlier. Then-U.S. Central Command (CENTCOM) chief General John Abizaid was quoted by *TIME Magazine* in November 2003 as stating that "the enemy has learned to adjust to our tactics, techniques and procedures".[52] This manifested in, *inter alia*, a rise in the use of remote detonation for improvised explosive devices (IEDs) and projectile attacks. This then removed the need to remain in close proximity to the detonation, thereby decreasing the chance to be found and detained. There was also an uptick in successful attacks against helicopters, usually by shoulder-fired RPGs and rockets.[53] It would be one of these RPGs, along with small arms fire, that targeted the convoy of Abizaid in Fallujah in February 2004 when it stopped outside the fortified Iraqi Civil Defense Corps building. He was unharmed.[54]

---

[49] Meijer, "'Defending our Honor'", p. 32.
[50] Brian Bennett, "Who are the Insurgents", *TIME Magazine*, 16 November 2003.
[51] Rory McCarthy, "Uneasy truce in the city of ghosts", *The Guardian*, 24 April 2004.
[52] Bennett, "Who are the Insurgents".
[53] Ibid.
[54] Jack Fairweather, "Top U.S. officer in Middle East escapes attack", *The Telegraph*, 13 February 2004.

Abizaid

Shortly after, on February 14, a large-scale and clearly coordinated daytime attack targeted near simultaneously three police stations, the mayor's office, and the Civil Defense Corps building. At just one of the sites, the attackers successfully released 20 prisoners.[55] Both of these events also followed the January deaths of two French nationals in a drive-by shooting that occurred after their car broke down just 13 kilometers (approximately eight miles) east of Fallujah.[56]

Amid the ongoing violence in Fallujah, it would be one event toward the end of March 2004 that proved to be the straw that broke the camel's back. On March 31, four U.S. private security contractors were ambushed in central Fallujah, and according to reports, their armored vehicle was first hit by an RPG, after which their bodies were set on fire and two were hung from a bridge that subsequently became known as "Blackwater Bridge".[57] It is believed that the four

[55] Patrick Graham, "23 killed as Iraqi rebels overrun police station", *The Guardian*, 15 February 2004 and Robert Hodierne and Robert Curtis, "Insurgents attack five sites, kill 17 Iraqi policemen", *Army Times*, 14 February 2004.

[56] Craig S. Smith, "The Struggle for Iraq: 2 French Citizens Are Killed by Gunmen on Iraqi Road", *The New York Times*, 7 January 2004.

[57] Paul Wood, "Iraq's hardest fight: The U.S. battle for Falluja 2004", *BBC News*, 10 November 2014 and "The High-Risk Contracting Business", *FRONTLINE*, 21 June 2005.

were killed by the initial RPG attack.

Military historian Bing West, who was quoted by the BBC's Paul Wood, stated that after this incident, Bush ordered that the city be seized.[58] The Bush administration harkened Fallujah to Somalia, implying that, this time, the U.S. wouldn't withdraw. This was a reference to former President Bill Clinton's evacuation of forces from Somalia after a Black Hawk helicopter was shot down over Mogadishu and the marines aboard ambushed and killed.[59]

This position contradicted the views of military commanders who preferred a less drastic approach involving the quiet apprehension of those deemed responsible for the private contractors' deaths. Among those who disagreed with an all-out offensive was Lieutenant General James Conway of the U.S. Marine Corps. "We felt like we had a method that we wanted to apply in Fallujah", he explained the following September in a piece that criticized the April 2004 operations, "that we ought to probably let the situation settle before we appeared to be attacking out of revenge".[60] Major General James Mattis similarly opposed such an operation, describing it as "exactly what the enemy wants".[61]

Despite these disagreements, the city was ordered captured, so the offensive began on April 2, with troops cordoning off the city and erecting checkpoints at its entrances and exits. Two days later, on April 4, the entire city was encircled and blockaded with a 19:00 to 06:00 curfew. Despite the cordon, reports indicated that anti-U.S. fighters were able to sneak into the city in preparation for the operation.[62] By that point, troops had also entered the industrial area located in the city's eastern outskirts and leaflets had been distributed instructing residents to abide by the curfew, remain inside as much as possible, and assist the arriving coalition forces with identifying insurgents.

The following day, on April 5, fighting commenced and the operation quickly ran into significant obstacles.[63] The subsequent fighting involved heavy urban warfare and hit-and-run guerrilla tactics, made more difficult for U.S. troops by their opponents' possession of more than just light arms. RPGs, IEDs, projectiles, and anti-aircraft guns were also frequently utilized.[64] "Marines I spoke to", wrote Paul Wood, the BBC journalist who was embedded with them during the Second Battle of Fallujah, "recalled being trapped, fired on from all sides".[65]

---

[58] Wood, "Iraq's hardest fight". See also Cottam and Huseby, *Confronting Al Qaeda*, pp. 43-4. For more on the role of private security contractors in Iraq, see Ann Scott Tyson, "Private Security Workers Living on Edge in Iraq", *The Washington Post*, 23 April 2005 and "The High-Risk Contracting Business", *FRONTLINE*.

[59] Meijer, "'Defending our Honor'", p. 32.

[60] Rajiv Chandrasekaran, "Key General Criticizes April Attack in Fallujah", *The Washington Post*, 13 September 2004.

[61] Interview with Mattis, as quoted in Cottam and Huseby, *Confronting Al Qaeda*, p. 44.

[62] Peace Direct and Oxford Research Group, "Learning from Fallujah", pp.8-9.

[63] "Marines, Iraqis join forces to shut down Fallujah", *CNN*, 6 April 2004 and Cottam and Huseby, *Confronting Al Qaeda*, p. 44.

[64] "Operation Vigilant Resolve", *GlobalSecurity.org*.

[65] Wood, "Iraq's hardest fight".

According to Corporal Christopher Ebert, who was quoted by the AP, fighters opposing the U.S. operation also refused to respond in the way that was expected. "Insurgents usually fire and run", he explained, "[but] this time they [were] digging in, which is the first time we've seen them do that".[66] It was reminiscent of the months leading up to this operation, in which, as previously discussed, insurgents were described as finding ways to adjust to U.S. tactics.

Although precision airstrikes supported ground fighting, they still caused damage and civilian casualties, which served to further inflame opposition to the U.S. presence among those who had remained in the city. This was likely exacerbated by the perception among at least some of the local population of the patronizing nature of the operation itself, which was described by coalition forces as "freeing" the city from thugs, criminals, Ba'athists, and foreign fighters. This is in addition to the fact that the entire event actually was, or at least appeared to be, retribution for the deaths of the contractors and for "being the symbol of an uprising that had shaken the U.S. occupation of Iraq to the core".

The issue of mosques being targeted was also particularly sensitive. On April 8, for example, it was reported that the U.S. used a missile and 500-pound bomb (approximately 227 kilograms) to target a group "of insurgents that were hiding behind the outer wall of a mosque, not the mosque itself".[67] Again, if locals believed that the mosque was, in fact, the target, the U.S. account, even if true, is irrelevant because it only contributed to local opposition.[68]

By April 9, the U.S. troops fighting in Fallujah were given the order to cease combat. By this time, reports indicated that they had captured somewhere between 25-67% of the city.[69] As far as casualties were concerned, as of April 13, 39 U.S. soldiers had been killed, as had an estimated 600 enemy fighters.[70] The truce was ordered in the interest of pursuing negotiations that involved a political delegation from the Sunni Iraqi Islamic Party (IIP), which was part of the governing council, as well as local Fallujah leaders and representatives of the resistance.[71] The ceasefire also allowed for humanitarian aid and other supplies to be distributed within the city,[72] for the dead to be buried, and for women, children, and the elderly to escape from the conflict. Men of fighting age, however, were banned from leaving.[73] On the Iraqi side, demands included a complete U.S. withdrawal from the streets leading into Fallujah; the repair of the city's main hospital; and the restoration of water, electricity, and other basic services. In exchange, a police force comprised of locals (i.e. Sunnis from Fallujah and surrounding areas) would handle the city's security. The U.S., for their part, called for the handover of all heavy weapons, such as

---

[66] Jonathan Steele, "Scores die as clashes spread", *The Guardian*, 7 April 2004.
[67] Jonathan Steele, "Battles rage from north to south", *The Guardian*, 8 April 2004.
[68] Naji Haraj, "The U.S. Treatment of Fallujah: the Fallujan View", May 2005 as quoted in Peace Direct and Oxford Research Group, "Learning from Fallujah", p. 15.
[69] Cottam and Huseby, *Confronting Al Qaeda*, p. 44 and Head, "The Battles of Al-Fallujah", pp. 110-11.
[70] Jonathan F. Keiler, "Who Won the Battle of Fallujah?", *The Naval Institute: Proceedings*, January 2005.
[71] "Operation Vigilant Resolve", *GlobalSecurity.org.*
[72] "Marines, Iraqis join forces to shut down Fallujah", *CNN.*
[73] Rory McCarthy, "Nine killed in U.S. convoy as Shia militias fight on", *The Guardian*, 10 April 2004.

RPGs and anti-aircraft guns; the removal of foreign fighters from the city; the return of Iraqi officials to engage in local governance; and the apprehension and surrender of those involved in the March killings of the four private security contractors.[74]

---

[74] McCarthy, "Uneasy truce in the city of ghosts" and Jonathan Steele, "Americans 'drop demand for handover of killers in Falluja atrocity'", *The Guardian*, 14 April 2004.

Pictures of Marines in combat during the First Battle of Fallujah

Despite the truce, which was extended on April 12, and a preliminary agreement that was reached by April 20,[75] the situation remained volatile. At the end of that month, for example, Fallujah saw three days of fighting involving gun battles between insurgents and U.S. forces, as well as air and artillery support in the form of precision airstrikes and cannon fire from gunboats.[76] Regardless of the violence, authorities insisted that the ceasefire still held.

At the very end of April, the U.S. military announced that it intended to withdraw from the city or, as a spokesman for described it, a "reposition".[77] Per one of the demands from the negotiations, security was to be taken over by a newly formed brigade comprised of former Iraqi soldiers and policemen, the majority of who were from Fallujah or nearby areas and which included at least some men who had fought against U.S. forces.

This brigade was to be led by former Saddam Hussein-era generals (first Jasim Muhammad Saleh and then Muhammad Latif). This was in direct contradiction to the policies that timed to exclude former members of the security services, but it was likely seen as a preferred option to the alternative of having militant Islamists advocating for conflict against foreign troops. Known as the "Fallujah Brigade" or "Fallujah Protective Army", it was an experimental unit established and armed by the U.S. and composed of between 1,000 to 1,100 men.[78]

---

[75] Luke Harding, "U.S. reaches deal with leaders in Falluja", *The Guardian*, 20 April 2004.

[76] Rory McCarthy, "Gunships pound Falluja despite ceasefire claims", *The Guardian*, 29 April 2004.

[77] John Kifner and Edward Wong, "The Struggle for Iraq: Security; Marines Transfer Falluja Positions to an Iraqi Force", *The New York Times*, 1 May 2004.

[78] George Wright and agencies, "U.S. forces to pull out of Fallujah", *The Guardian*, 29 April 2004; Kifner and

However, the goal of providing security in lieu of U.S. forces that had withdrawn was never realized. Rather, the experiment failed spectacularly, as elements from this brigade were largely found to be either actively or passively supporting anti-U.S. elements. This also meant that "the 800 AK-47 assault rifles, 27 pickup trucks and 50 radios the Marines gave the brigade wound up in the hands of the insurgents, according to Marine officers". Men wearing the uniform of this brigade also reportedly fired upon Marine-manned checkpoints.[79]

The failure of the Fallujah Brigade allowed the city to become a safe zone for anti-U.S. elements, including members of al-Qaeda in Iraq's predecessor, which implemented Islamic law. According to Roel Meijer, this was about the time when the nationalist, tribal, and religious rhetoric was increasingly supplanted by Salafist doctrine. He describes it as due to a "shift in power": "As [Fallujah] became dependent on the *mujahidin*[80] for its defence, it was this group, in alliance with radical *ulema*,[81] that was able to assume power form the more moderate tribal and religious leaders and supplant a discourse of tribal honour and religious nationalism with a discourse of Salafi radicalism."[82] Toward the end of May, for example, the sale of alcohol, drugs, and "morally depraved compact disks" were banned. Later, playing dominoes and shaving beards was also reportedly prohibited.[83] According to BBC's Paul Wood, "locals spoke of beheadings in the street".[84]

It is also worthwhile to note one event during this period that would particularly affect attitudes among the local population toward foreign troops. At the end of April 2004, what would become known as the Abu Ghraib prison scandal broke. This involved the release of photographs depicting the physical and sexual abuse of Iraqi detainees by U.S. servicemen and women at the detention facility in Abu Ghraib, located east of Fallujah and just west of the capital. Not long after, Major General Antonio Taguba released a report on his investigation into the 800th Military Police Brigade, which was responsible for detainee operations in Iraq at that time. In it, he detailed a long list of physical and sexual abuse, including the "videotaping and photographing naked male and female detainees" and the "forcibl[e] arrang[ement of] detainees in various sexually explicit positions for photographing".[85]

The scandal played a major role in fostering even more negative attitudes toward U.S. forces. For those in a city like Fallujah who were already opposed to the U.S. invasion, the revelations of sexual and physical abuse at the Abu Ghraib prison only solidified their opposition. The scandal was the epitome of humiliation.

Wong, "Marines Transfer Falluja Positions"; and Chandrasekaran, "Key General Criticizes".
[79] Chandrasekaran, "Key General Criticizes".
[80] This is the plural for mujahid, which refers to an individual who is engaged in jihad, or holy war.
[81] Literally translated into "the learned ones", it refers to those recognized as being scholars of and authorities in Islamic law and theology.
[82] Meijer, "'Defending our Honor'", p. 37.
[83] Ibid., p. 39.
[84] Wood, "Iraq's hardest fight".
[85] "Iraq Prison Abuse Scandal Fast Facts", *CNN*, updated 12 March 2016.

Chapter 4: Al-Qaeda in Iraq

The importance of al-Qaeda in Iraq (AQI) to the Second Battle of Fallujah cannot be overstated. In fact, the use of Fallujah as its base of operations and the presence of the group's leadership in the city was one of the primary justifications for the November 2004 offensive.

By that point, AQI's predecessor had declared allegiance to al-Qaeda and was responsible for a number of prominent attacks and executions across the country. Perhaps more importantly, the presence and operations of the militant jihadist group in Fallujah helped to more closely tie the 2003 invasion to the U.S. "war on terror". After all, it was Colin Powell himself who asserted there was a crucial link between Saddam Hussein's regime and al-Qaeda in the person of al-Zarqawi.[86]

When the U.S. first invaded in 2003, AQI did not yet exist, but its immediate predecessor did: This was a militant group known as Jama'at al-Tawhid w'al-Jihad ("Group of Monotheism and Jihad" and hereafter JTJ), which was formed in 1999 and led by al-Zarqawi, a Jordanian national. Ironically, al-Zarqawi and Osama bin Laden could not have differed much more than they did. Bin Laden grew up the son of a wealthy and successful construction magnate with ties to the Saudi royal family, whereas al-Zarqawi was born and raised in one of the poorest quarters of Zarqa in Jordan. Bin Laden attended an elite secondary school in Jeddah[87], while al-Zarqawi was heavily involved in crime during his teenage years, including dealing drugs in a dilapidated town cemetery that his house overlooked.[88] Bin Laden attended King Abdulaziz University in Jeddah to study economics, where he began studying religion fervently, but al-Zarqawi dropped out of secondary school, drank heavily, and covered his body with tattoos, earning him the nickname "Green Man," as both alcohol and tattoos are considered *haram* (sinful) in orthodox Sunni Islam.[89] Though bin Laden first decided to take up arms and wage violent *jihad* while participating in the fight against the Soviets in Afghanistan, al-Zarqawi had been arrested numerous times for shoplifting, mugging, drug dealing, sexual assaults, and drunken fights since his teenage years.

l-Zarqawi first went to Afghanistan in 1989, where he trained in one of al-Qaeda's camps before returning to Jordan in 1993. There, he formed a group led by himself and two other men, one of whom was the militant Salafist cleric Abu Muhammad al-Maqdisi, whose goal "was to overthrow the monarchy and establish an Islamic government". Al-Zarqawi's participation in this group led to his 1994 prison sentence, where a lot of his time was spent recruiting among the inmates and presenting his vision of Islam and *jihad*, or holy war.

As part of a general amnesty, he was released in 1999 and traveled again to Afghanistan, where

---

[86] "Full text of Colin Powell's speech", *The Guardian*.
[87] Lawrence Wright, *The Looming Tower: Al-Qaeda and the Road to 9/11* (New York: Random House, 2006), 78.
[88] Darwish, "Abu Musab Al-Zarqawi."
[89] Ibid.

he was given seed money from al-Qaeda to establish a training camp near Herat. This was despite disagreements with bin Laden, particularly with regard toward Shiites, all of whom al-Zarqawi considered legitimate targets. This disagreement over strategies is why al-Zarqawi did not pledge allegiance to bin Laden earlier; though he enjoyed the support of and funds from bin Laden, he did not consider himself an al-Qaeda member. He followed no orders, and he set up the Herat camp so that he could prepare people to go back to Jordan to carry out suicide missions.

In December 2001, after having fought since October against the U.S. invasion of Afghanistan, al-Zarqawi and hundreds of fighters from his training camp moved operations to Iran and the Kurdish autonomous region of northern Iraq. Although seemingly contradictory, given al-Zarqawi's perception of Shiites and Iran's status as majority Shiite, there is extensive research into the relations between the two, including theories that Tehran offered assistance to the group in order to mitigate the threat of attack on Iranian soil.[90] More importantly, as far as many reports are concerned, Powell's description of al-Zarqawi as the solid link between al-Qaeda and Saddam Hussein was highly questionable.[91]

After the U.S. invasion of Iraq, al-Zarqawi began conducting attacks against U.S. forces, its international allies, local "collaborators", and Shiites, ultimately moving his operations outside of Kurdish territory and Iran.[92] Some of the most notable and large-scale attacks occurred in August 2003. That month, a truck bomb detonated outside the Jordanian Embassy in Baghdad on August 7.[93] On August 19, another truck bomb exploded at the UN headquarters in Iraq's capital,[94] while a car bomb targeted the Imam Ali Shrine in Najaf, located south of Baghdad, at the end of the month on August 30. Among the over one hundred deaths from that attack was a prominent Shiite cleric, Ayatollah Mohammad Baqir al-Hakim. Al-Hakim was the leader of the Supreme Council of the Islamic Revolution in Iraq (SCIRI), a Shiite Islamist party.[95] In fact, the suicide bomber in the Najaf attack was reportedly al-Zarqawi's father-in-law.[96]

In her article on al-Zarqawi, *The Atlantic* reporter Mary Anne Weaver attributes the rise of his prominence to the scale and success of the August attacks, as well as U.S. rhetoric regarding al-

---

[90] For more on this, see Bruce Riedel, "The Al Qaeda-Iran connection", *The Brookings Institute*, 29 May 2011.

[91] Mary Anne Weaver, "The Short, Violent Life of Abu Musab al-Zarqawi", *The Atlantic*, July/August 2006. Weaver provides a well-written and well-researched account of his life. See also Aaron Y. Zelin, "The War between ISIS and al-Qaeda for Supremacy of the Global Jihadist Movement", *The Washington Institute for Near East Policy Research Notes*, No. 20, June 2014.

[92] Peter Grier and Faye Bowers, "Iraq's bin Laden? Zarqawi's rise", *The Christian Science Monitor*, 14 May 2004 and "Guide: Armed groups in Iraq", *BBC News*, 15 August 2006.

[93] Dexter Filkins, "At least 11 Die in Car Bombing at Jordan's Embassy in Baghdad", *The New York Times*, 7 August 2003.

[94] "Top UN official among dead in Baghdad blast", *The Guardian*, 19 August 2003.

[95] "Najaf bombing kills Shiite leader, followers say", *CNN*, 30 August 2003 and Bobby Ghosh, "The Forgotten Bombing That Ushered in an Age of Sectarian War", *The Atlantic*, 28 August 2015. The Imam Ali Shrine is believed to be the resting place for the first Shia Imam and fourth Sunni Caliph.

[96] Weaver, "The Short, Violent Life".

Zarqawi and the threat posed by his operations.[97] One of al-Zarqawi's goals was to ignite sectarian conflict by targeting Shiite holy sites and leaders. This aim was exemplified by the aforementioned Najaf attack, as well as the series of bombings in March 2004 that targeted Shiite commemorations for Ashura, a holy day that marks the martyrdom of the Islamic Prophet Muhammad's grandson and the first Shiite Imam.[98] Such a sectarian conflict, it was believed, believing that this would push the U.S. out of the country. Shiites were also perceived as apostates and, in September 2004, al-Zarqawi "issued an audiotape declaring 'total war' on Iraq's Shiite population".[99]

Letters later recovered at a raided al-Qaeda safe house have shown that al-Zarqawi was in frequent contact with bin Laden between 2003 and 2004. Al-Zarqawi was working to secure bin Laden's approval for his actions in Iraq, which demonstrated al-Zarqawi's realization that his network was only one of many different militant groups operating in Iraq – both Shiite and Sunni – and he needed the support and funds of a more powerful organization to give him the backing he needed to emerge as the top player on the Iraqi battlefield. On April 5, 2004, al-Zarqawi wrote in a letter to bin Laden that he had only two options: stay in Iraq and continue fighting U.S. and Coalition forces while also confronting the opposition of some Iraqis to his methods, or leave Iraq in search of another country to wage *jihad*. Days later, on April 9, 2004, he and his supporters kidnapped and beheaded U.S. national Nicholas Berg and then broadcasted the brutal execution on the Internet, and analysis of the video suggests it was al-Zarqawi himself who conducted the beheading.

In October 2004, just one month prior to the Second Battle of Fallujah and despite his disagreements with al-Qaeda regarding the targeting of Shiites, JTJ declared its allegiance to bin Laden and the al-Qaeda organization. The declaration that was released claimed that JTJ had been in communication with al-Qaeda eight months earlier, prior to the First Battle of Fallujah. JTJ thus became known as al-Qaeda in Iraq,[100] which would also be the predecessor to ISIS. Bin Laden accepted the pledge and welcomed al-Zarqawi and his network into the folds of al-Qaeda. A message posted on a website around that time announced, "Numerous messages were passed between 'Abu Musab' (Allah protect him) and the al-Qaeda brotherhood over the past eight months, establishing a dialogue between them. No sooner had the calls been cut off than Allah chose to restore them, and our most generous brothers in al-Qaeda came to understand the strategy of the Tawhid wal-Jihad organization in Iraq, the land of the two rivers and of the Caliphs, and their hearts warmed to its methods and overall mission. Let it be known that al-Tawhid wal-Jihad pledges both its leaders and its soldiers to the mujahid commander, Sheikh 'Osama bin Laden' (in word and in deed) and to jihad for the sake of Allah until there is no more

[97] Ibid.
[98] "Deadly attacks rock Baghdad, Karbala", *CNN*, 2 March 2004.
[99] Emily Hunt, "Zarqawi's 'Total War' on Iraqi Shiites Exposes a Divide among Sunni Jihadists", *The Washington Institute*, 15 November 2005.
[100] "Al-Zarqawi group vows allegiance to bin Laden", *AP*, 18 October 2004.

discord and all of the religion turns toward Allah...By Allah, O sheikh of the mujahideen, if you bid us plunge into the ocean, we would follow you. If you ordered it so, we would obey. If you forbade us something, we would abide by your wishes. For what a fine commander you are to the armies of Islam, against the inveterate infidels and apostates!" Ironically, while JTJ's allegiance to al-Qaeda was done despite disagreements regarding Shiites, it would be this and other issues that led al-Qaeda to publicly break with ISIS in 2014.

It would be a mistake, however, to attribute al-Zarqawi and AQI's rise solely to the former. Rather, the circumstances on the ground helped create an ideal atmosphere for the Sunni militant jihadist group. Not only was the population Sunni, they were quite dissatisfied and angered by U.S. actions in Iraq. In other words, instead of al-Zarqawi and his initial band of fighters being an al-Qaeda group, it was the U.S. invasion of Iraq that gave al-Zarqawi the opportunity to consolidate his network, amass his power, and establish formal ties with al-Qaeda. The war gave him the chance to confront not just the near enemy, but also the far enemy simultaneously. Just like the Soviet occupation of Afghanistan gave bin Laden and his early supporters the perfect battleground to gain popularity and gather strength, the Iraq War was key in the development of al-Zarqawi's group from a loosely structured network of militant fighters into an organized, well-funded, and well-equipped army that fought not just Coalition forces but rival militants, particularly those from Shiite brigades.

The connection with al-Qaeda further empowered al-Zarqawi. He now enjoyed greater credibility and legitimacy that came with being part of the al-Qaeda band, and his group's increasing popularity led to a steady flow of funds, arms, and fresh recruits. In turn, bin Laden gained as well; al-Qaeda had been suffering operationally following its ejection from Afghanistan after 9/11, so al-Zarqawi represented the fighting figurehead bin Laden needed to regain al-Qaeda's momentum.

Chapter 5: The Second Battle of Fallujah

Ahead of the offensive in late 2004 and following the failed battle in April, attacks targeting coalition troops based around Fallujah continued alongside frequent airstrikes within the city. There were four airstrikes in the city, for example, between June 19 and July 5 that targeted safe houses linked to al-Zarqawi and his affiliates.[101] By mid-September, U.S. strikes were occurring on a daily basis, particularly against suspected JTJ cum AQI positions.[102] These would continue until the start of operations and continue throughout the offensive.

There were a number of reasons for a second offensive against Fallujah. The first was related to an interest in finding and detaining al-Zarqawi, who was using the city as his base of operations. Al-Zarqawi's group had also been involved in the assassinations of foreigners,

---

[101] Rebecca Leung, "U.S. Strike in Fallujah Kills 10", *CBS News*, 5 July 2004.
[102] Rory McCarthy, "Daily U.S. bombing raids seen as anticipating all-out Falluja attack", *The Guardian*, 20 September 2004.

including British engineer Ken Bigley[103] and South Korean national Kim Sun-il.[104] In fact, some accounts describe the final straw in negotiations as the demand for locals to handover al-Zarqawi. Local officials described this as an "impossible condition".[105] Thus, although negotiations had officially continued even after the failure of the Fallujah Brigade with the aim of restoring local governmental control, these finally collapsed in mid-October/early November.

Another reason was increasing pressure to restore order and reduce violence in the Sunni majority Fallujah ahead of planned national elections in January 2005. Iraqi prime minister Ayad Allawi warned that "an assault to retake the territory was imminent".[106] Prior to the commencement of the operation, civilians were warned to leave Fallujah, while any individual suspected of links to insurgents was detained at the checkpoints erected around the city.[107] The situation was described as a siege that was laying the groundwork for another offensive to take the city.

On October 18 Iraq's national security advisor, Kassim Daoud, "insisted [...] that there would be an offensive against the city unless militants were handed over",[108] referring to al-Zarqawi and other foreign fighters affiliated to him. Paul Wood also explained that, by October, journalists who would be embedded with the forces tasked with capturing the city arrived at Camp Fallujah. They were part of a strategy aimed at refuting allegations regarding the destruction of mosques during the first battle of Fallujah. Journalists were to refute claims that they were destroyed without provocation. According to the military, they were frequently used as "insurgent bases", with minarets a popular spot for snipers and weapons caches often found inside. In the absence of such conditions, the U.S. military insisted that mosques would never be targeted.[109]

---

[103] Agencies, "U.S. forces continue strikes on Falluja", *The Guardian*, 15 October 2004.
[104] "South Korean hostage 'beheaded'", *AP*, 22 June 2004.
[105] Agencies, "U.S. forces continue strike".
[106] James Glanz, "Attack Kills 15 as Allawi Warns Falluja Rebels", *The New York Times*, 1 November 2004.
[107] Wood, "Iraq's hardest fight".
[108] Jamie Wilson, "Death toll climbs as Falluja siege continues", *The Guardian*, 19 October 2004.
[109] Wood, "Iraq's hardest fight".

Allawi

In addition, immediately ahead of the offensive, which officially began just after dusk on November 9, Allawi declared a 60-day state of emergency and implemented various security measures. This included a round-the-clock curfew in Fallujah, a warning to locals against carrying weapons, as well as the closures of highways, the border crossings with Syria and Jordan, and Baghdad International Airport.[110] At the time of the offensive, estimates widely vary at to the number of people remaining in the city, with some citing approximately 100,000[111] and others putting the number lower at between 30,000 and 50,000.[112] Over a million leaflets were dropped on the city calling on residents not to fight in the upcoming battle and to remain indoors.[113] Reconnaissance aircraft also patrolled the sky above Fallujah, taking aerial photos that would assist in the identification of targets and execution of precision air strikes.[114]

---

[110] Rory McCarthy, "U.S. troops enter Falluja as jets pound rebel-held city", *The Guardian*, 9 November 2004
[111] Ibid.
[112] Rory McCarthy and Peter Beaumont, "Civilian cost of battel for Falluja emerges", *The Guardian*, 14 November 2004.
[113] Robert Worth, "Sides in Falluja fight for Hearts and Minds", *The New York Times*, 17 November 2004.
[114] Head, "The Battles of Al-Fallujah", p. 112.

The Second Battle of Fallujah was also known as both Operation Al Fajr ("the dawn") and Operation Phantom Fury, and it spanned from November 7 to December 24, 2004. This battle, often considered the climactic clash of the Iraq War, would come well over a year after Bush had announced the end of "major combat operations in Iraq." Participating in these operations were between 10,000 and 15,000 U.S. troops, as well as five Iraqi battalions, or about 2,000 soldiers.[115] According to Jonathan Keiler, a former captain in the U.S. Army's Judge-Advocate General Corps (JAG), "the actual assault element comprised about 6,000 U.S. troops in four Marine battalions [...] and Army Task Force 2-2 (two mechanized battalions)". Aircraft and several artillery battalions from the Army and Marine Corps also participated.[116] Meanwhile, about 850 British forces—members of the British Black Watch Battalion—participated in the city's encirclement and cordon and were tasked with preventing any movement of fighters between Fallujah and other cities, including Ramadi to the east and Baghdad to the west.[117]

On the opposing side, there are conflicting figures as to the number of insurgents who remained in the city. Prior to the start of the offensive, some estimates put the number at 5,000, while others believed that between 2,000 and 3,000 insurgents were in the city at the start of the battle.[118] Some accounts even attempted to distinguish between the fighters, describing "500 "hardcore" and 2,000 "part time" insurgents,[119] likely referring to trained militants like al-Zarqawi and the more localized resistance comprised of armed Iraqis.

Although accurately determining such numbers is difficult, the discrepancy can likely be explained by reports that a substantial number of fighters had fled Fallujah, al-Zarqawi himself. Some reports indicated that they simply moved locations ahead of the offensive, with Ramadi cited as one possible destination. By the fall of 2004, Ramadi had seen a notable increase in violence, including the specific targeting, through kidnappings and assassinations, of important local officials deemed as collaborators. In July 2004, for example, three sons of the Anbar Province governor were kidnapped in Ramadi.[120] When it came to fighting in Fallujah, therefore, the force that U.S. and Iraqi troops ultimately faced was believed to be a "rearguard" of sorts, with the militants' goal being to bog down and target the attacking forces.[121]

According to Paul Wood's account, Lieutenant Colonel Gary Brandl, who led the 1st Battalion, 8th Marine Regiment, described the battle plan as "an old fashioned marine charge". This meant that "one rifle company would take the main road into Fallujah. A second would go up that road to move into the complex of government buildings in the centre".[122] Another account of the

---

[115] McCarthy, "U.S. troops enter Falluja" and Michael Ware, "The Brutal 2004 Siege of Fallujah", *TIME Magazine*, 22 November 2004.
[116] Keiler, "Who Won the Battle of Fallujah" and Head, "The Battles of Al-Fallujah", p. 112.
[117] McCarthy, "U.S. troops enter Falluja".
[118] Keiler, "Who Won the Battle of Fallujah".
[119] Head, "The Battles of Al-Fallujah", p. 113.
[120] Pamela Hess, "Iraqi official's children kidnapped", *UPI*, 29 July 2004.
[121] Ware, "The Brutal 2004 Siege".
[122] Wood, "Iraq's hardest fight".

offensive described it as a "two-pronged push by marines into suburbs in the north, while U.S. army soldiers fired volleys of mortars into the southern parts of the city".[123] This meant that the first neighborhoods to see combat were the al-Jolan neighborhood (sometimes referred to as Golan) in the northwest and the al-Askari neighborhood in the northeast.

Despite the relatively simple descriptions of the battle plan, the Second Battle of Fallujah was anything but simple or "old fashioned". Much like the April operation, it involved heavy urban warfare and guerilla fighting, described as "block-by-block, street-by-street" fighting that aimed to steadily clear individual buildings.[124] Some accounts even detailed "room to room" fighting in each of the buildings. This was done with substantial artillery and air support. In fact, Rebecca Grant, an air power expert, described operations in Fallujah as "mark[ing] the unveiling of an urban-warfare model based on persistent air surveillance, precision airstrikes, and swift airlift support".[125] One obstacle related to the latter, however, involved the use of surface-to-air missiles (SAMs) among the insurgents. Dr. William Head, a historian and author of *The Battles of Al-Fallujah: Urban Warfare and the Growing Roles of Airpower*, explained that gunships, such as the fixed wing Lockheed AC-130s, operated "almost totally at night" due to concerns about SAMs.[126]

The style of fighting was also deadly. In just the first few days of the offensive, 24 U.S. servicemen were killed and over 200 wounded.[127] Unsurprisingly, given the presence of AQI-affiliated elements, part of the challenge was the use of IEDs, mines, and booby-trapped buildings. In one account described by Michael Ware, an embedded journalist from *TIME Magazine*, a wire was found running into a nearby house during operations aimed at capturing a series of buildings in Fallujah in November. In that nearby house, gas cans, a car battery, and a propane tank were discovered rigged to explode.

In the days that followed, members of the 3rd Platoon "found countless bombs, plus doors booby trapped and walls set with explosives". In another instance, an attempt to rout as many as 150 fighters from a mosque in the al-Askari neighborhood saw the U.S. bomb a weapons cache, which then "set off a daisy chain of roadside bombs for 100 yards (approximately 92 meters) along either side of the block". Blast walls and other barriers were also often set up by anti-U.S. fighters as a means of controlling and directing the movement of attacking troops.[128] On top of all that, tunnels, trenches, and spider holes were prepared ahead of the offensive to allow for greater ease of movement by insurgents. All of these techniques would be replicated in the years to come: After the insurgents were cleared from cities across Iraq, the painstaking and gradual

[123] McCarthy, "U.S. troops enter Falluja".
[124] Joshua Steward, "Remembering Fallujah 10 years later", *Military Times*, 7 November 2014.
[125] Rebecca Grant, "The Fallujah Model", *Air Force Magazine*, February 2005 as quoted in Head, "The Battles of Al-Fallujah", p. 115.
[126] Ibid, p. 114.
[127] Ware, "The Brutal 2004 Siege".
[128] Ibid.

process of clearing IEDs, booby traps, and mines would always be required, while underground tunnel networks were a frequent discovery as well.

Despite the obstacles and casualties, the first few days also saw relatively swift success, with advancing forces quickly capturing two strategic bridges and steadily moving south from the northern neighborhoods until Highway 15, which cuts across the city horizontally at the middle, was captured. This "opened the way for more forces to pour into the center of Fallujah and advance toward the south of the city".[129] By the early evening hours of November 9, all power had been cut to the city[130] and, only three days later on November 12, 80 percent of the city was described as under control by U.S. and pro-U.S. forces.[131]

The southern parts of the city, however, were some of the last and more difficult areas to retake. Fallujah's Risala and Nazzal neighborhoods, for example, saw heavy resistance.[132] "An underground bunker and steel-enforced tunnels connecting a ring of houses filled with weapons, medical supplies and bunk beds" were discovered in an unspecified area of the city's south. Fighters were also described as dressed in "full military battle gear", while U.S. equipment and ready-to-eat U.S. meals were found.[133] This suggested that some or all of the fighters in the city's south were former members of the failed Fallujah Battalion that aimed to bring local security enforcement to the city, but which ultimately saw its members support the insurgency.

The next day, on November 13, the majority of the city was described as under control, with the next steps involving a "house-to-house mop sweep". This sweep, which was estimated to require four to six days for completion, began two days later, on November 15, [134] a day after the city was officially declared as "liberated". This declaration was made despite pockets of fighting that still occurred in areas of the city, at least some of which were likely attributed to the "sweep". In fact, as of November 14, Captain Erik Krivda, a member of Task Force 2-2, was quoted as stating that 90 percent of the city was recaptured with the remaining ten percent described as the "most difficult".[135] This likely referenced the southern neighborhoods, which had yet to be fully ousted and which also contributed to continued violence in the city. Instead, the former JAG captain Jonathan Keiler cites November 20 as the date that this was completed.[136]

Despite the inaccurate declaration, November 15 did mark the starting point for humanitarian efforts. By mid-November, Fallujah General Hospital was reopened, medical equipment was dispatched, and members of the Red Crescent began arriving to negotiate with authorities on the

---

[129] Ibid.
[130] Head, "The Battles for Al-Fallujah", p. 116.
[131] Jackie Spinner and Karl Vick, "Troops Battle for Last Parts of Fallujah", *The Washington Post*, 14 November 2004.
[132] Head, "The Battles of Al-Fallujah", p. 116.
[133] Spinner and Vick, "Troops Battle for Last Parts".
[134] Head, "The Battles of Al-Fallujah", p. 117.
[135] Spinner and Vick, "Troops Battle for Last Parts".
[136] Keiler, "Who Won the Battle of Fallujah?"

distribution of humanitarian aid.[137]

Even years after the Second Battle of Fallujah was fought, the number of casualties still differ. Some accounts state that 82 coalition and six Iraqi soldiers were killed and 600 coalition and 52 Iraqi soldiers injured. [138] Other accounts report 51 killed and 425 "seriously wounded," with Iraqi forces suffering eight deaths and 42 injuries.[139] The U.S. military also estimated that 2,000 insurgents were killed and 1,200 captured, [140] out of the 2,000-5,000 estimated be in the city at the start of the fighting.

With regard to physical damage, this was extensive but, again, numbers conflict. Reports indicate that between 9,000 and 10,000 homes were destroyed completely or deemed unsafe to inhabit, with thousands more damaged. [141] One report put the number of damaged homes at half of the 39,000 in the city,[142] while another stated that as many as 60 schools and 65 mosques in "the city of mosques" were damaged or destroyed.[143]

Despite the aforementioned pockets of continued fighting, the official commencement of resettlement of internally displaced persons (IDPs) commenced on December 23, 2004. This description, however, is misleading, because on that day, 900 residents, the vast majority of which were from the al-Andalus neighborhood of western Fallujah, were not resettled but were permitted to only briefly enter the city to "see the condition of their homes and decide if they want to move their families back".[144] Those who would decide to return would receive a stipend that amounted to approximately $100, along with food aid and kerosene. Those whose homes were completely destroyed would be given the equivalent of $10,000 in compensation. Returning residents would be required, at least initially, to retrieve water by hand from the 24 temporary water tanks set up in lieu of the damaged water infrastructure. Men of military age were also required to register for identification cards that included retinal and fingerprint scans and could be swiped at checkpoints.[145]

Like the battle itself, the timing of the reconstruction effort was directly connected to the upcoming national elections, with authorities hoping to convince the country's minority Sunni population to vote. Among other reasons, a low turnout from this segment of the population would reduce the election's legitimacy and publicly demonstrate a lack of trust in Iraq's

---

[137] "Humanitarian efforts set to begin in Falluja", *CNN*, 14 November 2004.
[138] Dan Lamothe, "Remembering the Iraq War's bloodiest battle, 10 years later", *The Washington Post*, 4 November 2014.
[139] Keiler, "Who Won the Battle of Fallujah?".
[140] Lamothe, "Remembering the Iraq War's bloodiest battle".
[141] Jim Miklaszewski, "Still locked down, Fallujah slow to rebuild", *NBC News*, 14 April 2005 and Ann Scott Tyson, "Increased Security in Fallujah Slows Efforts to Rebuild", *The Washington Post*, 19 April 2005.
[142] Tyson, "Increased Security in Fallujah".
[143] Dahr Jamail, "Iraq: Life Goes On in Fallujah's Rubble", *Inter Press Service*, 23 November 2005.
[144] Erik Eckholm and Eric Schmitt, "The Conflict in Iraq: Rebuilding; Invited Home, 900 Evacuees Revisit Fallujah", *The New York Times*, 24 December 2004.
[145] Ibid.

leadership and democratic process. Concerns regarding voter participation among this population were clearly demonstrated by the Sunni IIP's withdrawal from the interim government in direct response to the offensive. The Muslim Scholars Association, which was composed of Sunni clerics and represented 3,000 mosques, had also called for a boycott of the January elections.[146] In addition to its delegitimizing factor, low turnout would be fodder for militant Sunni jihadist groups like AQI.

Despite the interest in expediting resettlement and reconstruction, the process was slow. By April 2005, far less than half of the city's population had returned, with one number putting it as low as 90,000.[147] In addition, out of 32,000 claims for compensation by homeowners, only 2,500 had been paid. Residents were also angry at the amount of the compensation; one local was described by an NBC News reporter as having received only 20% of the value of his home. In addition, only half the remaining homes in the city had working electricity, and telephone service was described as almost nonexistent.[148]

The security situation was also less than ideal. NBC News quoted Major Mark Gurganus in April 2005 as explaining that "by keeping the city under a little tighter control at this point, we can prevent those guys [the insurgents] from coming back". However, the measures described constituted more than just "a little tighter". That month, the city was depicted as being "still in almost total lockdown. Traffic backs up for house as every vehicle is searched before entering the city. And there [was] still an overnight curfew". [149]

Part of the reason was the continued threat of attacks. Earlier in April, five roadside bombs were discovered in Fallujah,[150] while the following June, six military personnel were killed when a U.S. convoy was targeted by a suicide car bomb.[151]

Naturally, the security concerns also served to slow down the city's reconstruction. *The Washington Post* reporter Ann Scott Tyson described a situation in which four Iraqi men "of military age" who were living together in one house were subject to an arrest raid. However, rather than operating a militant safe house, they were part of a 78-member crew hired to help build a new sewerage system in the city. Their detainment meant that work on the sewerage system had to be paused: The project manager stated that the four men were heavy equipment operators and essential to the job. Tight checkpoints also delayed the entry of material into Fallujah, which caused high prices for in demand products, particularly food and fuel. [152] All of this, along with the absence of an official local government, slowed down both physical

[146] "Operation al-Fajr (Dawn) and Operation Phantom Fury [Fallujah], *GlobalSecurity.org* and Head, "The Battles for Al-Fallujah", p. 116.
[147] Tyson, "Increased Security in Fallujah".
[148] Miklaszewski, "Still locked down".
[149] Ibid. See also, Tyson, "Increased Security in Fallujah".
[150] Miklaszewski, "Still locked down".
[151] "Four Women Are Among Six U.S. Servicemen Killed in Fallujah Attack", *Fox News*, 24 June 2005.
[152] Tyson, "Increased Security in Fallujah".

reconstruction and that of the economy. One only needs to recall one of the factors that led to the insurgency - the expulsion of many Sunni men from the country's security services -to understand the dangers of high unemployment. In April 2005, Captain Rudy Quiles, a civil affairs officer, estimated unemployment and underemployment combined was around 85 percent.[153] In essence, the ability to provide tight security would be meaningless if the absence of income and slow rebuilding process pushed locals to fight against the U.S. presence.

Tactically speaking, the Second Battle of Fallujah was largely considered to be a success, but strategically there was no victory. If one of the goals was to recapture the city from insurgents, then this was achieved, though it did not occur as quickly as officials wanted to believe (i.e. not on November 14). By the end of December, when efforts to resettle IDPs officially commenced, pockets of fighting continued to be reported in the city. If another aim was to strike a blow[154] against AQI and capture al-Zarqawi, a reasonable assumption given the demand from the April 2004 negotiations to turn him over, then the operation was a major failure. In fact, in mid-November, AQI "leaders claimed that 90 percent of the group's fighters had left the city and that the remaining 10 percent had been killed".[155] And if one of the aims was to provide security to the Sunni population in Fallujah and encourage their support of the U.S. invasion and participation in the national elections, this was likely also a failure. There was extensive damage to the city, involving both the destruction of buildings, as well as infrastructure for services like water and electricity. Although some accounts of the destruction were exaggerated and included claims that entire blocks had been leveled, there was still substantial and extensive damage.[156] Put simply, the results of the fighting and the portrayal of the situation added to the existing resentment among the local population specifically and the broader Iraqi population more generally.

[153] Ibid.
[154] Spinner and Vick, "Troops Battle for Last Parts".
[155] Spinner and Vick, "Troops Battle for Last Parts".
[156] Keiler, "Who Won the Battle of Fallujah?"

Chapter 6: The Impact and Aftermath of the Battle

The impact of the Second Battle of Fallujah was not limited to the city itself. Although one of the goals of the battle was to clear insurgents, particularly fighters linked to AQI, from the city, insurgent attacks were also stepped up outside of the city ahead of and during this period. This strategy, which would be continued by AQI's successor, the Islamic State (also known as the Islamic State of Iraq and al-Sham or ISIS), aimed to divert resources and attention away from Fallujah, continue efforts to ignite further sectarianism, and demonstrate the militant group's strength even in the face of a U.S. offensive. Indeed, on November 9, the day that the operation commenced, two suicide vehicle-borne improvised explosive devices (a fancy name for a suicide car bomb) detonated outside two churches in Iraq's capital. A Baghdad hospital, which was reportedly treating victims from the church bombings, also came under attack by mortar fire that day, while a U.S. convoy en route to the airport was also targeted by a suicide attack.[157]

Alongside an uptick in asymmetric attacks, the Second Battle of Fallujah has also been described as triggering a spread of fighting across the country between coalition forces and insurgent forces. By November 16, reports indicated that clashes had also been reported in Ramadi, the provincial capital of the Anbar Province located west of Fallujah; Baqubah, the provincial capital of the Diyala Province; Mosul, the provincial capital of the northern Nineveh Province; Suwayra, which is located southeast of Baghdad in the Wasit Province; Buhriz, about 22 miles (approximately 35 kilometers) northeast of the capital, also in the Diyala Province, and in areas of the country's capital.[158]

The operation to take Fallujah also become one of the rallying calls and recruitment tools for armed opposition to foreign forces thanks allegations of U.S. atrocities against the local population and symbols of Islam. *Al-Jazeera* was occasionally accused of presenting a distorted picture of the situation in Fallujah; according to *The New York Times* journalist Robert Worth, the network "endlessly repeat[ed] video clips of events like what appeared to be the shooting this week of an injured Iraqi prisoner in a Falluja mosque". Inaccurately elevated casualty numbers and the previously mentioned allegations that whole blocks had been leveled also served as topics for recruitment efforts.[159]

During and following the offensive, as is often the case particularly with urban warfare, various allegations regarding actions taken by the U.S. military and allied Iraqi forces surfaced. Of course, it was and remains hard to determine the validity of each side's claims given the fog

---

[157] McCarthy, "U.S. troops enter Falluja"; "Rebels attack Baghdad, N. Iraq", *CNN*, 9 November 2004; and Omar Sinan, "Bombings rock Iraqi capital; 6 people die", *AP*, 9 November 2004.

[158] Rory McCarthy, "Fighting spreads to more towns as Falluja operation continues", *The Guardian*, 16 November 2004.

[159] Worth, "Sides in Falluja".

of battle and the type of warfare fought in Fallujah.

Perhaps the most notable point of contention was that men of fighting age were barred from leaving the city ahead of the offensive, although other civilians, including women, children, and the elderly were. These charges stated that, despite reports regarding tens of thousands of residents that remained in the city, U.S. forces acted as if the only remaining inhabitants were fighters.[160] The U.S. military, on the other hand, denied such accusations and pointed to the distribution of flyers ahead of the campaign, and warnings to civilians to remain in their homes and against the taking up of arms. They also pointed to various efforts aimed specifically at reducing casualties among the population, including the use of precision airstrikes.

A lengthy report by the Internal Displacement Monitoring Centre (IDMC) released in May 2006 included a section that covered "allegations of violations of international human rights and humanitarian law" in Fallujah in 2004. These primarily focused on the delivery of aid and situation of civilians that had remained in the city once the offensive commenced. The report quoted IRIN, a provider of humanitarian-focused news and analysis, as describing difficulties faced by non-governmental organizations (NGOs) in delivering food, medical supplies, and other aid to residents that remained in Fallujah. The U.S. military, for their part, explained certain prohibitions and limitations on entry into the city as due to concerns for the safety of the aid convoys. The IDMC's report also notes that the UN Assistance Mission for Iraq (UNAMI) issued various statements regarding the status of civilians in Fallujah, emphasizing that any accusations regarding the "deliberate targeting of civilians, indiscriminate and disproportionate attacks, the killing of injured persons and the use of human shields" must be investigated. UNAMI further questioned the access and provision of aid to civilians in Fallujah and IDPs at their various camps. [161]

In another report, this time released in January 2005, the Studies Center for Human Rights and Democracy in Fallujah (SCHRD) detailed what they described as "American crimes in al-Fallujah" between November 7 and December 25, 2004. This report forwarded a number of accusations, including claims that U.S. forces and its Iraqi allies captured Fallujah General Hospital shortly after the invasion commenced and physically restrained doctors, stole equipment, and arrested all the patients.[162] In a report about Fallujah by Ali Fadhil, an Iraqi doctor, some of these accusations were repeated. Fadhil repeats a description of the early days of the invasion from a local physician from the city's main hospital, Dr. Adnan Chaichan: "He told me that all the doctors and medical staff were locked into the hospital at the beginning of the attack and not allowed out to treat anyone. The Iraqi National Guard, acting under U.S. orders, had tied him and all the other doctors up inside the main hospital. The U.S. had surrounded the

---

[160] See, for example, George Monbiot, "Behind the phosphorus clouds are war crimes within war crimes", *The Guardian*, 22 November 2005.

[161] "Iraq: Sectarian violence, military operations spark new displacement, as humanitarian access deteriorates", *Internal Displacement Monitoring Centre*, 23 May 2006, pp. 124-5.

[162] Head, "The Battles of Al-Fallujah", p. 115.

hospital, while the National Guard had seized all their mobile phones and satellite phones, and left them with no way of communicating with the outside world."[163]

SCHRD also alleged that two more hospitals were destroyed. Additional accusations mentioned in the report include ones of arbitrary arrests, killings of unarmed civilians, poor prison conditions, refusal to collect and bury dead bodies, purposeful destruction of mosques, theft and looting, subjective determination of compensation, and the use of chemical weapons.[164] Although it is unclear if U.S. authorities directly responded to the SCHRD report, similar allegations were persistently denied. In fact, historian William Head stated that an Iraqi battalion, the 36th Commando Battalion, took over Fallujah General Hospital in the initial days of the offensive in order to provide medical services. He also noted later accusations that the hospital had been used by insurgents to disseminate "false information on the number of civilian casualties".[165]

The SCHRD's accusations regarding chemical weapons were not unique. A documentary called "Falluja: The Hidden Massacre" broadcast on RAI, an Italian network, in November 2005, alleged that white phosphorous was used by U.S. forces in Fallujah. However, the evidence presented in the documentary was considered flimsy by other parties. One BBC report determined that the "second and third hand accounts" presented in the documentary "were simply not convincing enough for the BBC to start running the story". They further stated, among other critiques, that "the documentary sticks together a lot of different sequences from different places".[166] The U.S., which does not deem white phosphorous as a chemical weapon but rather an incendiary weapon used to light up parts of the battlefield and make it easier for forces to target enemy combatants, responded to initial allegations by stating that the substance was used only to illuminate battlefields in Iraq. Later, however, the U.S. was forced to reverse its position when, in November 2005, the April-March 2005 issue of *Field Artillery*, a U.S. Army journal, "surfaced on the Internet".[167] In one of the journal's articles discussing the Second Battle of Fallujah, the use of white phosphorous was described using WP as shorthand for the substance. The article said, "WP proved to be an effective and versatile munition. We used it for screening missions at two breeches and, later in the fight, as a potent psychological weapon against the insurgents in trench lines and spider holes when we could not get effects on them with HE [high explosive munitions]. We fired 'shake and bake' missions at the insurgents, using AP to flush them out and HE to take them out."[168]

---

[163] Ali Fadhil, "City of Ghosts", *The Guardian*, 11 January 2005.
[164] "A briefed report on American Crimes in Al-Fallujah for the period of November 7 to December 25, 2004", *Studies Center for Human Rights and Democracy in Fallujah*, 14 January 2005 (unofficial translation).
[165] Head, "The Battles of Al-Fallujah", p. 115.
[166] See "Heated debate over white phosphorous", *BBC* News, 17 November 2005 and Monbiot, "Beyond the phosphorous clouds".
[167] "Heated debate", *BBC News.*
[168] Captain James T. Cobb, First Lieutenant Christopher A. LaCour, and Sergeant First Class William H. Hight, "TF2-2 in FSE AAR: Indirect Fires in the Battle of Fallujah", *Field Artillery*, Mar.-Apr. 2005, p. 26 as quoted in "David P. Fidler, "The Use of White Phosphorus Munitions by U.S. Military Forces in Iraq", *American Society*

After this revelation, Pentagon spokesperson Lieutenant Colonel Barry Venable, denied that it was used against civilians in Fallujah but admitted its use "as an incendiary weapon against enemy combatants".[169]

Finally, Peace Direct and Oxford Research Group's 2005 report on the city presents "unused options" that could have been pursued at the various "milestones" in Fallujah, such as the lead up to the second battle. These "unused options" are actions that the report's authors argue could have been taken in order to prevent the actual outcome. Among other suggestions, it lists the retention of local officials and security offices in the city; methods of improving outreach to and communication with the local Sunni population; apologies and investigations into accusations of improper conduct and violence from coalition forces; swifter compensation to families; and proper burials, as opposed to leaving corpses on the street.[170]

Although the Second Battle of Fallujah was concluded by the end of 2004 and followed by reconstruction efforts, the story of the city was far from over at that point. A decade later, there would be major battles for Fallujah, and more rebuilding, but this time led by the reconstructed Iraqi military, as well as tribal and Shiite militias.

February 2005 witnessed what is often referred to as the unofficial start to the "Sunni Awakening". In that month, members of a Sunni tribe in al-Qaim, an Anbar Province town on the Syrian border, requested U.S. assistance in fighting against al-Qaeda.[171] By this time, elements among the Sunni population had become angered by some of the militant group's actions. This included growing perceptions that Iraqis were being attacked at the same rate or even more than foreign forces. Al-Zarqawi was not just waging a war against "invaders", he was specifically and frequently targeting Iraqi nationals. Although this included "collaborators", which meant anyone who was or believed to be working with the Iraqi government or foreign forces, the primary targets were Shiites.

Najim Abed al-Jabouri and Sterling Jenson identify additional reasons for increasing Sunni opposition to al-Qaeda. In addition to violence toward non-Sunni Iraqis, "symbols of Iraqi nationalism" also came under attack. Furthermore, al-Qaeda's "extreme behaviors and demands" alienated many Sunnis, such as those that "compel[ed] families to marry their daughters to suicide bombers [and] forc[ed] divorces for wives they desired". Another reason, they argue, was a changing perception of U.S. attitudes toward the Sunni population, including efforts that were being undertaken to reverse de-Ba'athification policies and reintroduce former officers and soldiers into the armed forces. There was also opposition to the increasing involvement of Iran.[172]

---

of International Law, Vol. 9, Issue 37 (6 December 2005).

[169] "U.S. used white phosphorus in Iraq", *BBC News*, 16 November 2005.

[170] Peace Direct and Oxford Research Group, "Learning from Fallujah".

[171] Najim Abed al-Jabouri and Sterling Jensen, "The Iraqi and AQI Roles in the Sunni Awakening", *Prism*, Vol. 2, No. 1 (December 2010): pp. 3-4.

[172] Ibid, pp. 9-10.

In 2006, the Anbar Awakening was officially announced. This was a coalition of Sunni tribes in the Anbar Province whose goal was to rout al-Qaeda-affiliated elements from the area. Most importantly, this was an initiative pursued with the support of local Sunni leaders, comprised of local Sunnis, and undertaken with support from U.S. forces. These efforts, which reversed some of the poor decisions made at the onset of the 2003 invasion, proved to be a success. By May 2007, reports indicated that there was a noticeable reduction of al-Qaeda's presence and attacks in the Anbar Province.[173]

This change in the course of the war also coincided with important events. In May 2007, President Bush declassified a U.S. intelligence report revealing that bin Laden had enlisted al-Zarqawi to plan strikes inside the U.S., and the report also warned that in January 2005, bin Laden had tasked al-Zarqawi with setting up a militant cell inside Iraq that would be used to plan and carry out attacks against the U.S.[174] Whether al-Zarqawi actually followed orders and established such a cell is unknown, but fortunately, he never came close to conducting attacks on U.S. soil because he was killed by an airstrike on June 7, 2006 in Baquba, Iraq.

Nonetheless, his legacy still resonates in Iraq, because his "martyrdom" skyrocketed his reputation; radical clerics cite al-Zarqawi's words and past actions to this day, and new militant groups have formed in his honor, such as the al-Zarqawi Brigades in Mauritania[175] and the al-Zarqawi group in Bajuar, Pakistan.[176] The living legacy of one of the darkest figures of the region's history is now very deeply rooted in the jihadist movements that are exploiting the breakdown in law and order across the Islamic and Arabic world today.

Al-Zarqawi's most obvious legacy is ISIS, which recaptured Fallujah, Ramadi, and other areas of the Anbar Province in early 2014. The group's shocking and very sudden success can be explained by a number of factors, but most notably the alienation of the Sunni population by Iraq's Shiite leadership. Immediately prior to its capture, for example, a Sunni protest camp in Ramadi was forcibly broken up. The camp, which was erected a year earlier, was condemning the perceived marginalization of the Sunni population in Iraq by the then-Prime Minister Nouri al-Maliki.[177] That came at the end of December 2013, and by the next month, Ramadi and Fallujah came under ISIS' control. On January 3, 2014, a local journalist was quoted by *The Washington Post* reporter Liz Sly as saying that "at the moment, there is no presence of the Iraqi state in Fallujah".[178]

In fact, after the U.S. withdrawal in 2011, it would be ISIS's expansion that truly brought

---

[173] Joe Klein, "Is al-Qaeda on the Run in Iraq", *TIME*, 23 May 2007.
[174] Dan Froomkin, "Failing to Reassure," *The Washington Post*, May 24, 2007,
   http://busharchive.froomkin.com/BL2007052401145_pf.htm.
[175] "Morocco's Militants," *The Economist*, Feb 21, 2008, http://www.economist.com/node/10733039.
[176] "Another Militant Group Opposes BISP," *The News*, April 10, 2009,
   http://www.thenews.com.pk/TodaysPrintDetail.aspx?ID=171651&Cat=7&dt=4/9/2009.
[177] Kamal Namaa, "Fighting erupts as Iraq police break up Sunni protest camp", *Reuters*, 30 December 2013.
[178] Liz Sly, "Al-Qaeda force captures Fallujah amid rise in violence in Iraq", *The Washington Post*, 3 January 2014.

substantial American forces back to Iraq. By the summer of 2014, after large swaths of territory in Syria and northern Iraq fell under ISIS control, the U.S. began conducting airstrikes against ISIS targets. In September of that year, an international anti-ISIS coalition was formed, and it continues to conduct such strikes in both Iraq and Syria.

One of the most recent chapters, but likely not the last, was the 2016 battle for Fallujah that commenced in May and concluded in June. Its goal was to reverse the 2014 takeover of the city by ISIS and involved the participation of Iraqi military and police forces, as well as Sunni and Shiite militias. It also came amid a rise in successful Iraqi- and Kurdish Peshmerga-led operations to roll back ISIS advances, including out of Ramadi.

As the past decade attests, there are many lessons to be taken from Fallujah, and especially from the events of 2004. The fighting demonstrated the limitations of foreign military operations in the absence of local support; the Second Battle of Fallujah may have been a tactical success, but the subsequent need for security lockdown and the difficulties faced during the process of reconstruction meant that, while the battle may have been won, the war was not. Ultimately, it would require a Sunni-led and Sunni-backed alliance to succeed in pushing AQI out of Anbar Province. In other words, absent support from the local population, the U.S. military in Fallujah mostly served to stoke sustained resistance, even if only inadvertently.

Fallujah in 2004 is also a story of failed policies and the ramifications of those policies. Although hindsight is always 20/20, it is fair to argue that policies in Fallujah that took into consideration the local population's perceptions, values, and concerns would have heralded different outcomes. Building upon the existing security forces rather than disbanding them and rethinking the policy of de-Ba'athification could have seriously altered the negative perceptions of the invading forces. Increased efforts to understand the local population and its values might have done the same, as would an Iraqi government that wasn't so closely linked to Iran and concretely addressed the concerns of the Sunni population.

For now, the city is out from under the thumb of ISIS, but as history has shown, it could easily rise as a bastion of resistance to the Iraqi government if policies mimic the mistakes of the past instead of furthering reconciliation. The withdrawal of Iranian-backed Shiite militias from Sunni populated areas, for instance, will almost certainly be necessary, as will a Sunni composition of local security forces and government. More importantly, the Iraqi government will need to actively engage the Sunni population and address their interests to stave off the possibility of history repeating itself.

Online Resources

Other books about Middle East history by Charles River Editors

Other books about Fallujah on Amazon

Bibliography

No True Glory: A Frontline Account of the Battle for Fallujah, by Bing West (2005) (ISBN 978-0-553-80402-7)

We Were One: Shoulder to Shoulder with the Marines Who Took Fallujah, by Patrick O'Donnell (2006) (ISBN 978-0-306-81469-3)

Fighting For Fallujah: A New Dawn for Iraq, by John R. Ballard (2006) (ISBN 978-0-275-99055-8)

Fallujah With Honor: First Battalion, Eighth Marine's Role in Operation Phantom Fury, by Gary Livingston (2006) (ISBN 1-928724-06-X)

Battle of Fallujah: Occupation, Resistance And Stalemate in the War in Iraq, by Vincent L. Foulk (2006) (ISBN 0-7864-2677-2)

Among Warriors In Iraq: True Grit, Special Ops, and Raiding in Mosul and Fallujah, by Mike Tucker (2006) (ISBN 978-1-59228-732-1)

Iraq 1941: The Battles For Basra, Habbaniya, Fallujah and Baghdad, by Robert Lyman (2006) (ISBN 978-1-84176-991-2)

My Men Are My Heroes: The Brad Kasal Story, by Brad Kasal as told to Nathaniel R. Helms (2007) (ISBN 0-696-23236-7)

On Call In Hell: A Doctor's Iraq War Story, by Cdr. Richard Jadick (2007) (ISBN 0-451-22053-6)

House to House: An Epic Memoir of War, by SSG David Bellavia (2007) (ISBN 978-1-4165-7471-2)

The Navy Cross: Extraordinary Heroism in Iraq, Afghanistan and Other Conflicts, by James E. Wise, Scott Baron (2007) (ISBN 1-59114-945-2)

Marakat Al-Fallujah: Hazimat Amrika Fi Al-Iraq, by Ahmad Mansur (2008) (ISBN 978-977-427-309-4)

Sunrise over Fallujah (2008) (ISBN 978-0-439-91625-7)

Fallujah: Shock & Awe (2009) (ISBN 978-0-85124-706-9)

Inside Fallujah: The War on the Ground, Ahmed Mansour (2009) (ISBN 978-1-56656-778-7)

The Daily Thoughts of a Fallujah Marine by Josh Daugherty (2009) (ISBN 978-1-60836-044-4)

Popaditch, Nicholas; Steere, Mike (2008). Once a Marine: An Iraq War Tank Commander's Inspirational Memoir of Combat, Courage, and Recovery. ISBN 978-1-932714-47-0.

Operation Phantom Fury: The Assault and Capture of Fallujah, Iraq, by Dick Camp (2009) (ISBN 978-0-7603-3698-4)

New Dawn: The Battles for Fallujah, by Richard S. Lowry (2010) (ISBN 1-932714-77-4) plus Presentation at the Pritzker Military Library on November 3, 2011

Free Books by Charles River Editors

We have brand new titles available for free most days of the week. To see which of our titles are currently free, click on this link.

Discounted Books by Charles River Editors

We have titles at a discount price of just 99 cents everyday. To see which of our titles are currently 99 cents, click on this link.